I0504914

AI HIP HOP COLORING BOOK

The prompt:

Yo, check it out, fam - we're talking 'bout AI drawing,
Creating images that got people jaw-dropping,
Got the power to make art that's straight up popping,
Using tech to get creative, and ain't no stopping.

For this prompt, we want an internet cash machine,
With style so fresh, it's fit for a king or queen,
Got the flow of a comedian, funny and mean,
Using AI drawing, creating a masterpiece scene.

So grab your spray paint and let's get to work,
We'll make this image stand out, make it jerk,
Add some humor and wit, give it some quirk,
With AI drawing, we'll make it berserk.

In hip hop graffiti style, we can make it fly,
With images so fresh, it'll reach for the sky,
AI drawing gives us the power to try,
Creating art that'll leave people mystified.

copyright 2023. All Rights Reserved. Jeremy Hubert Burt.

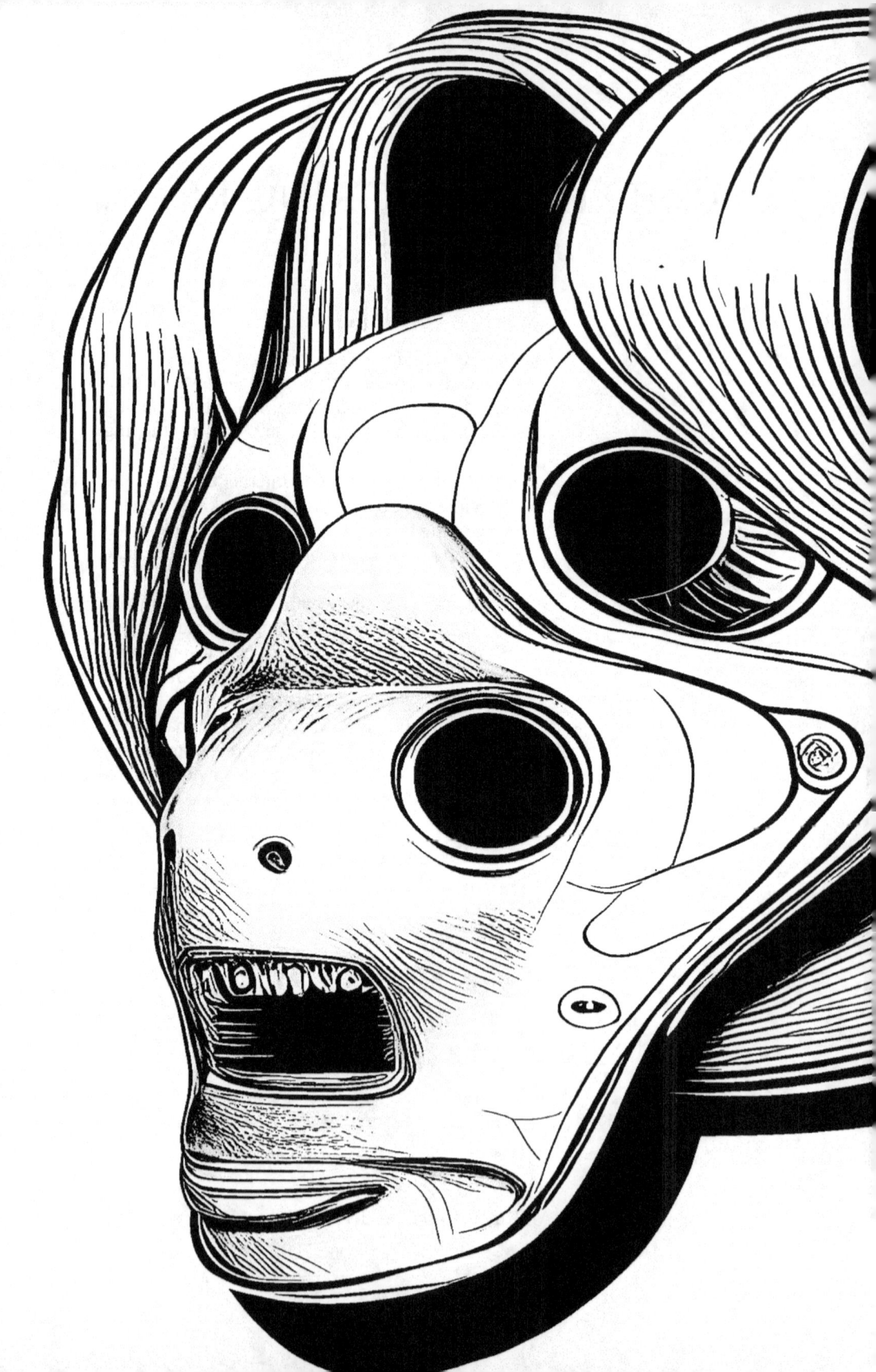

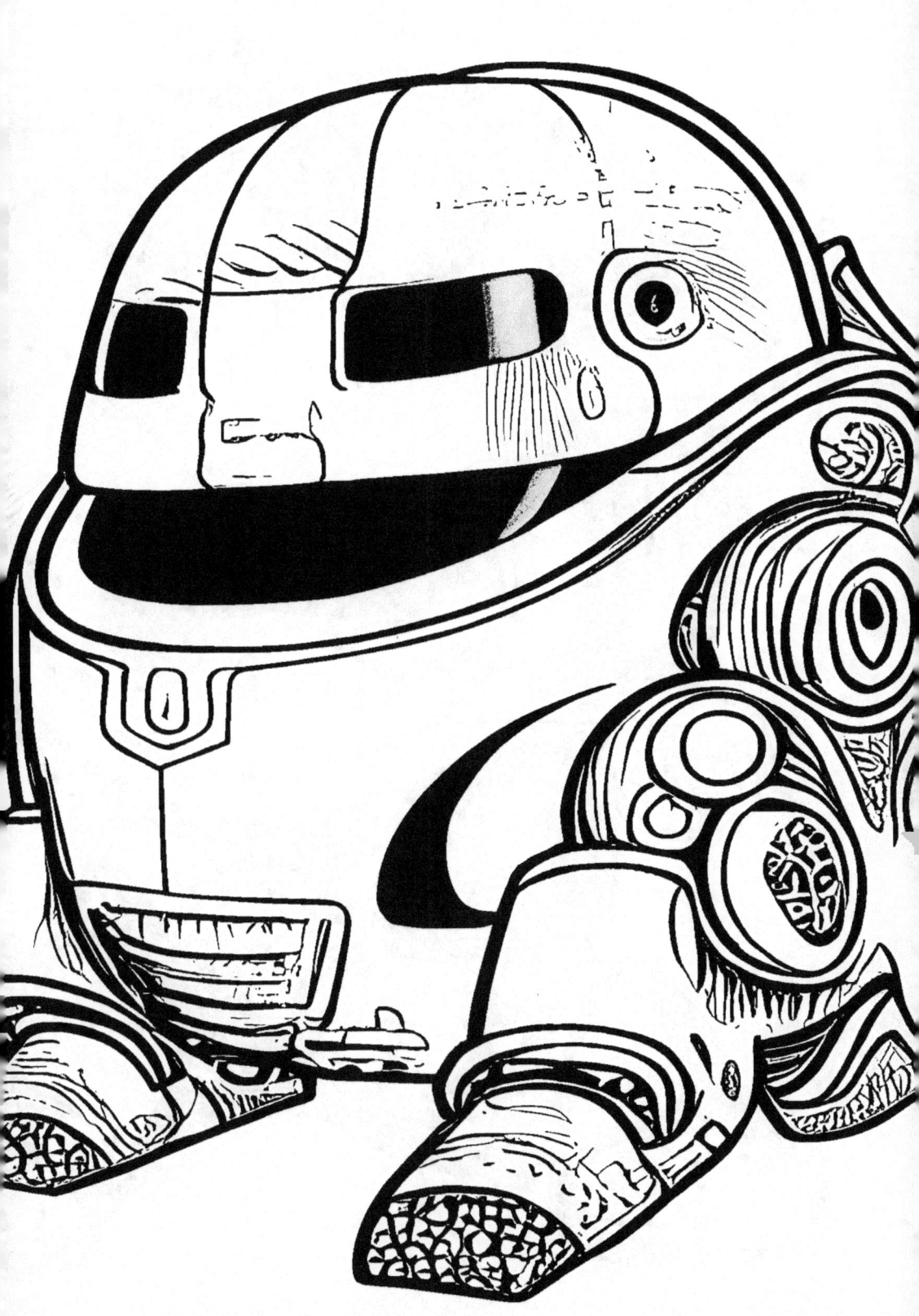

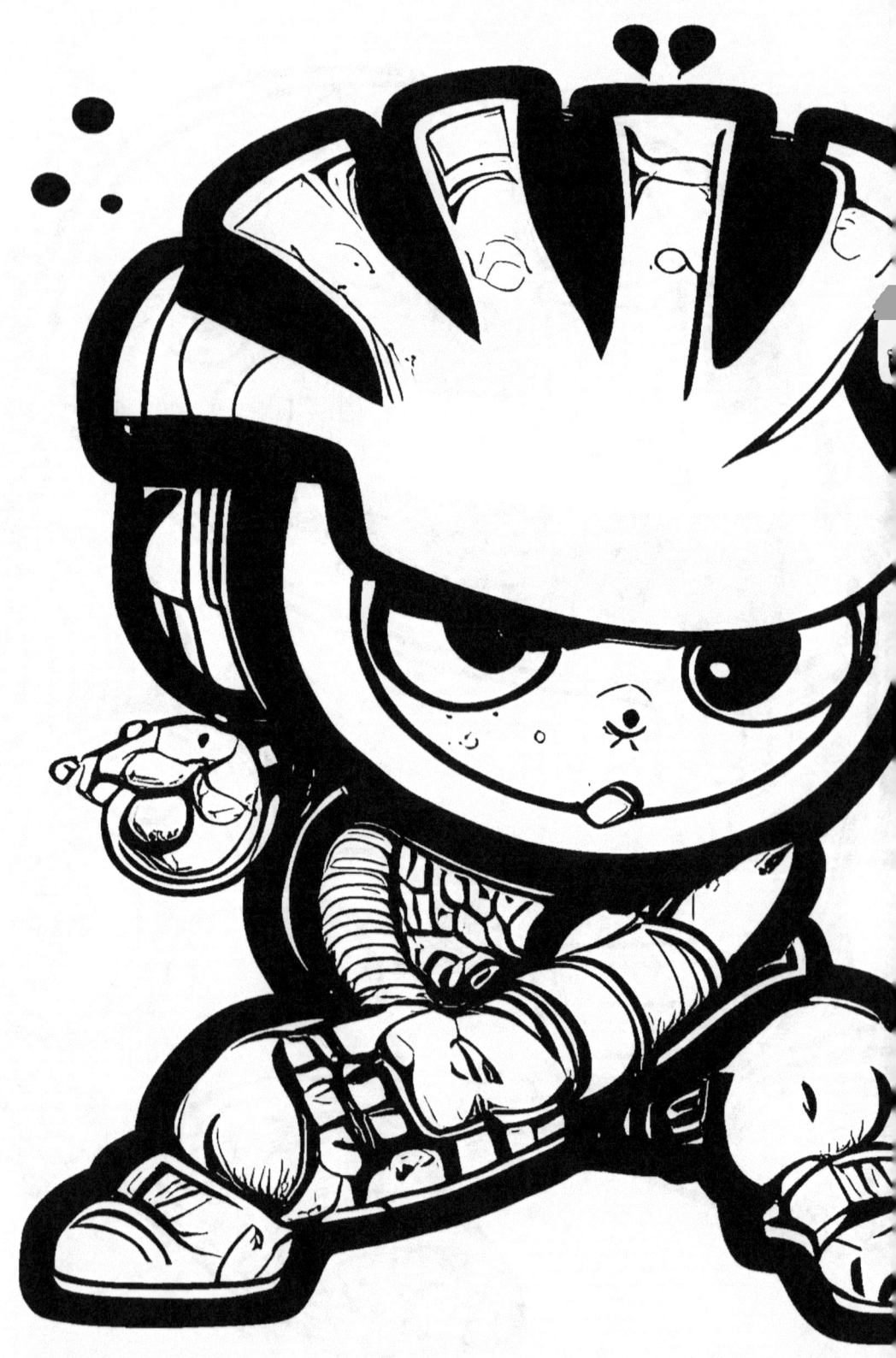

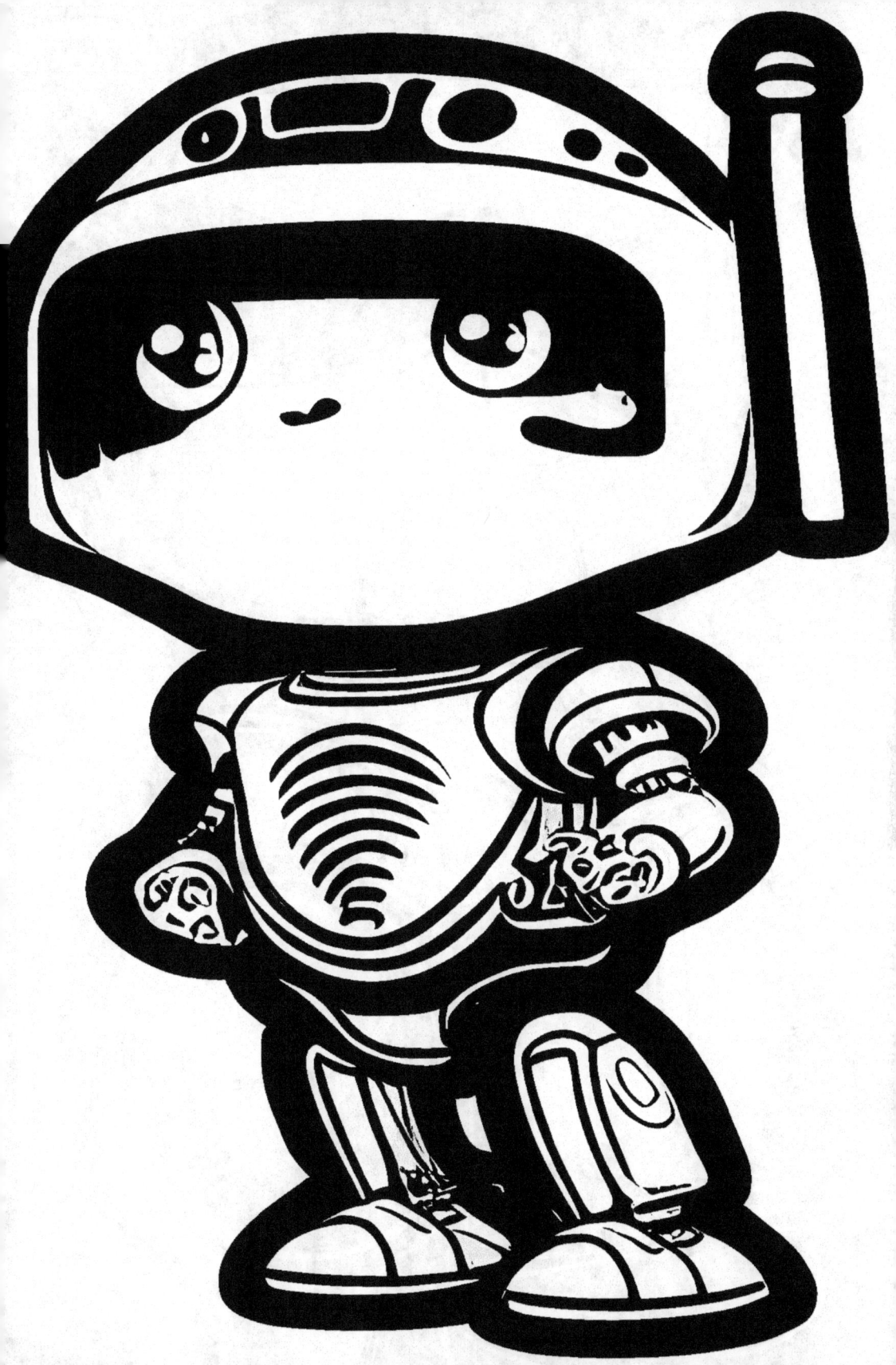

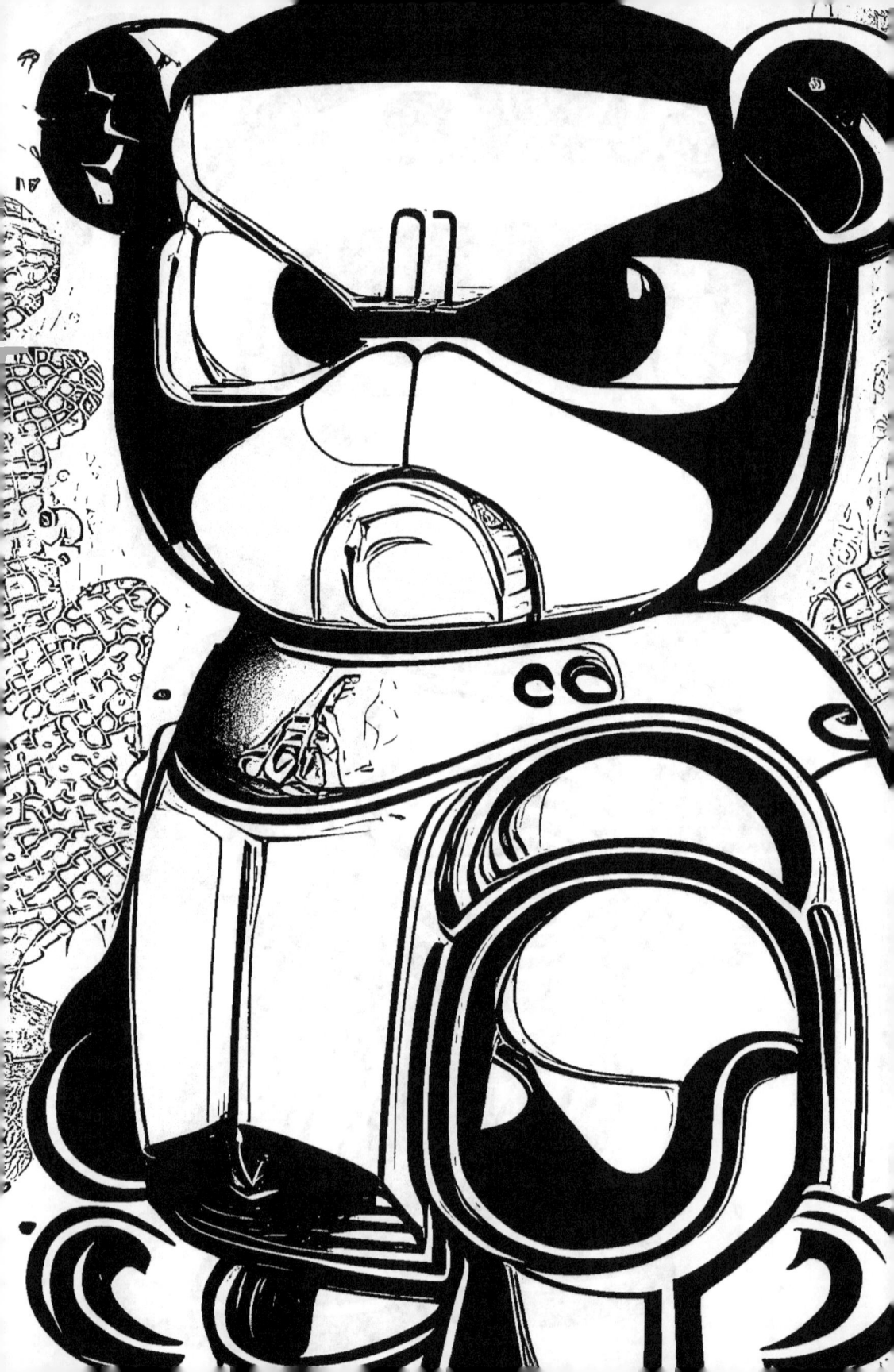

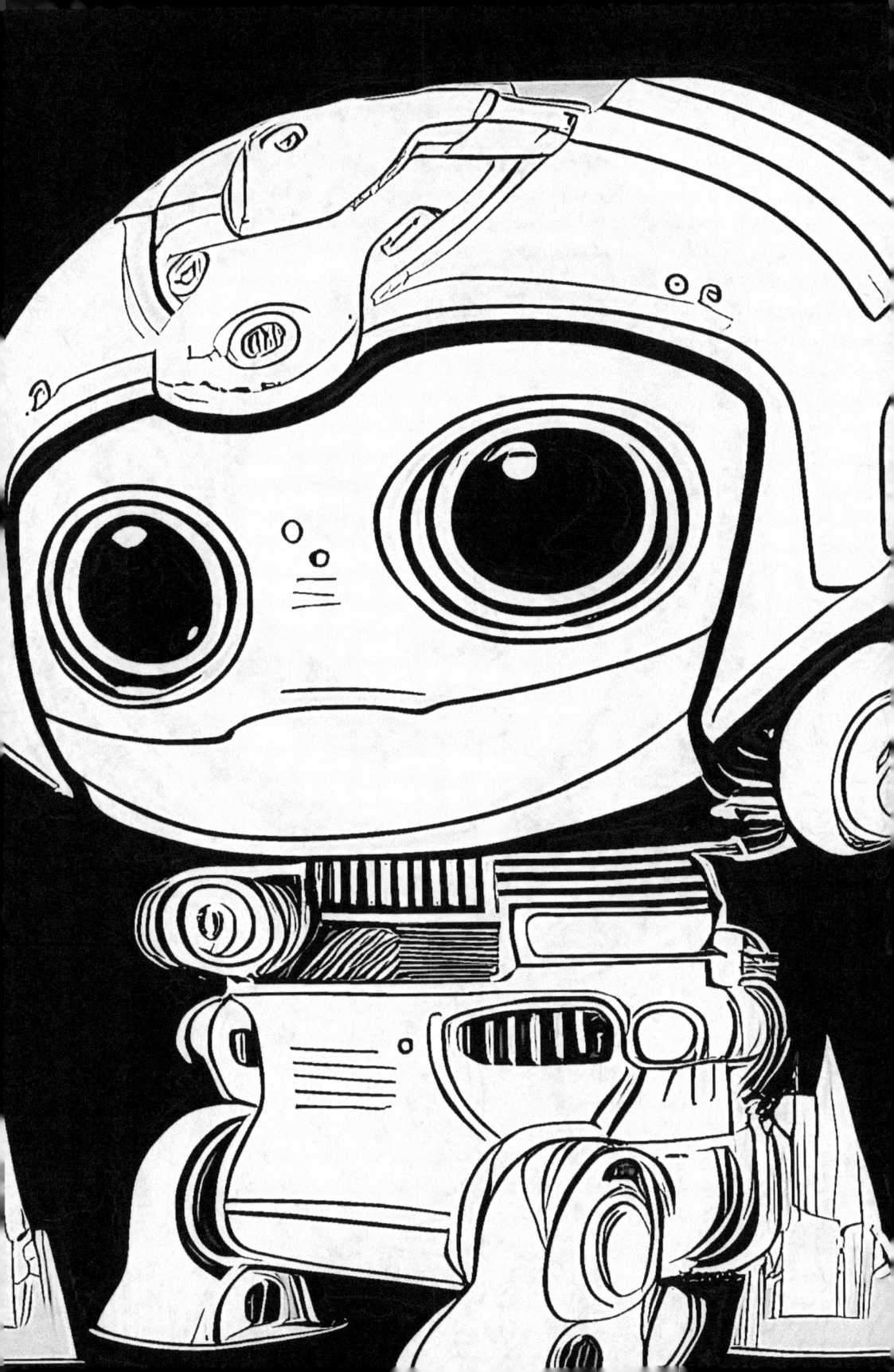

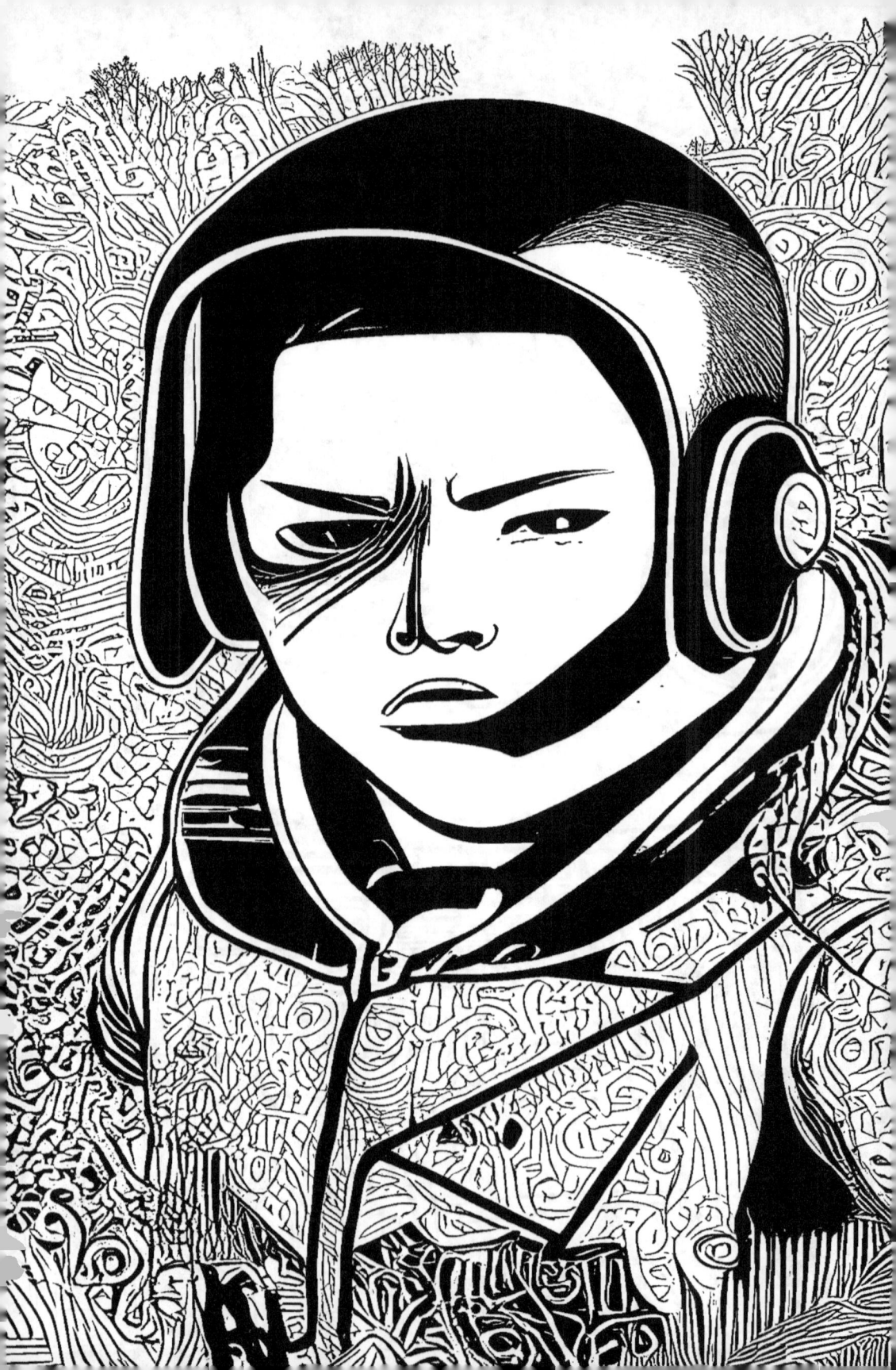

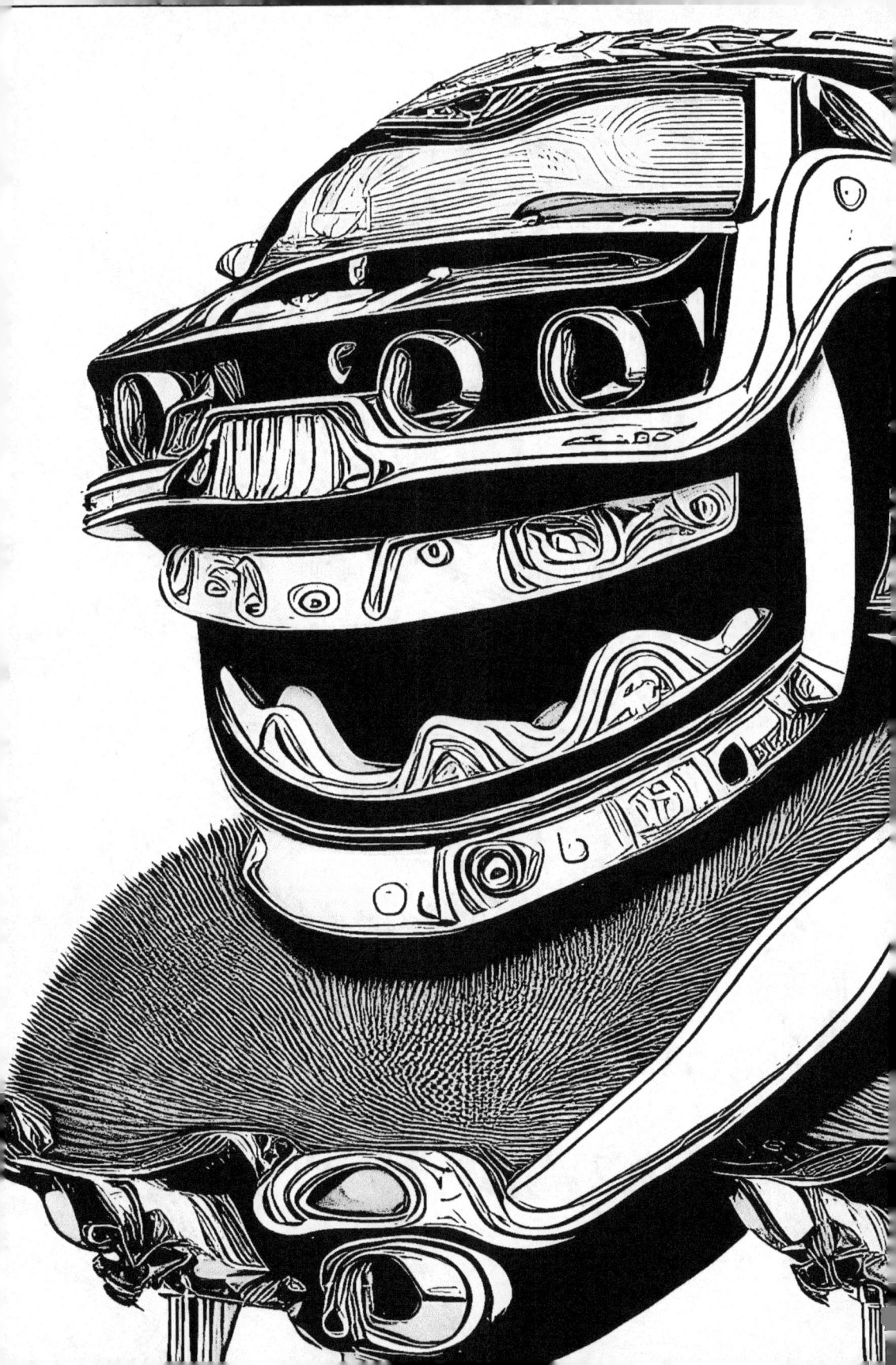

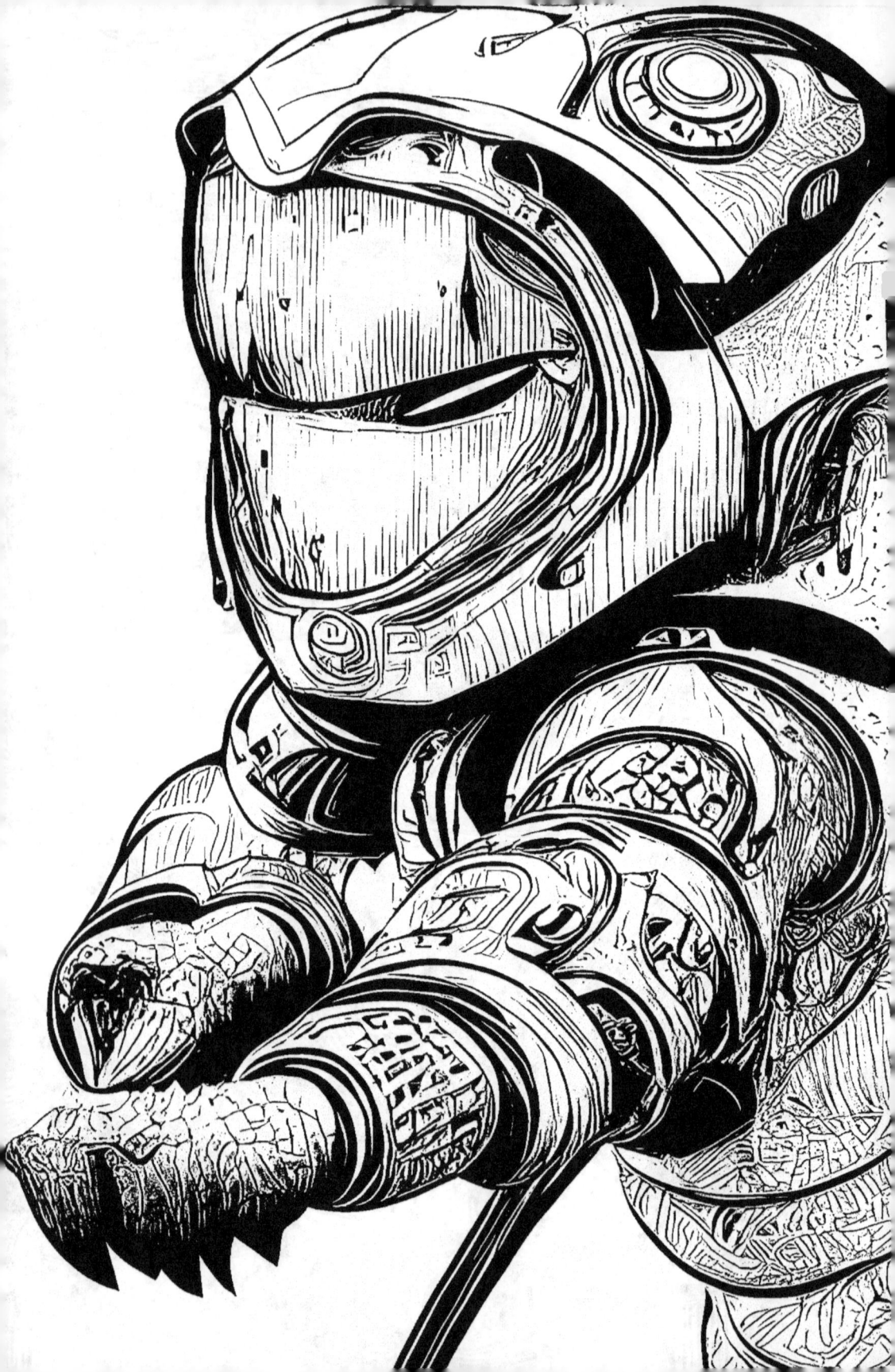

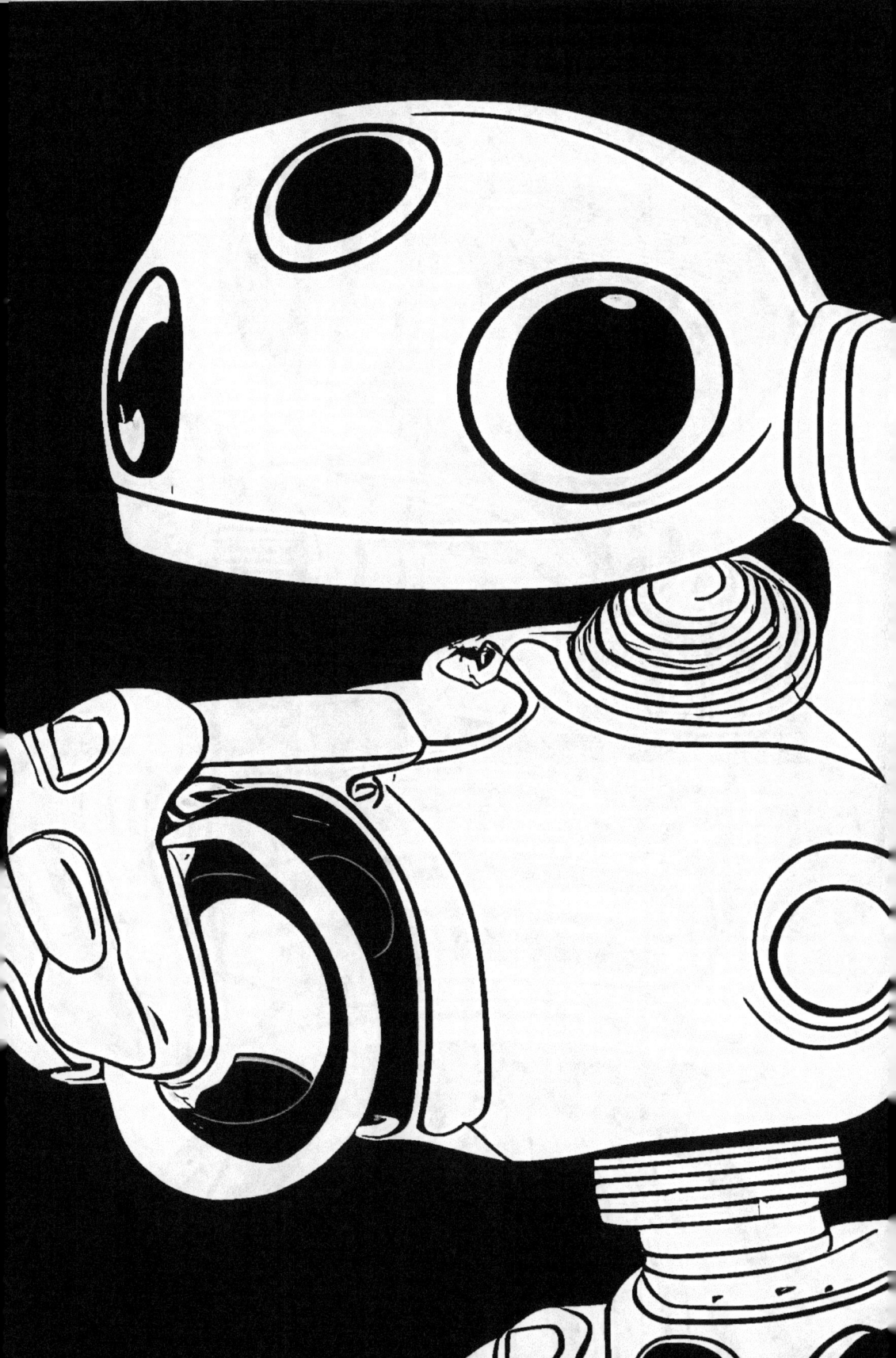

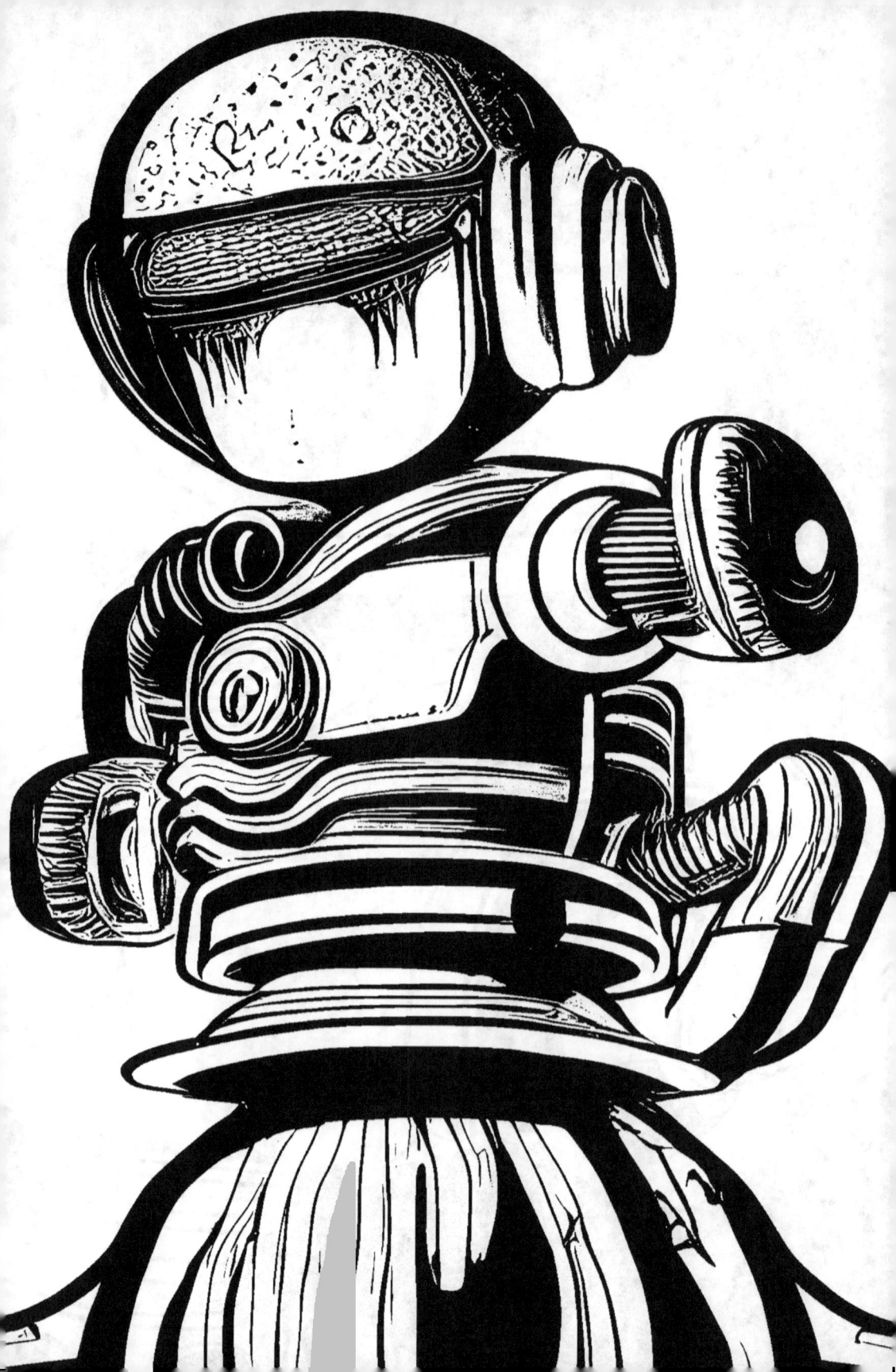

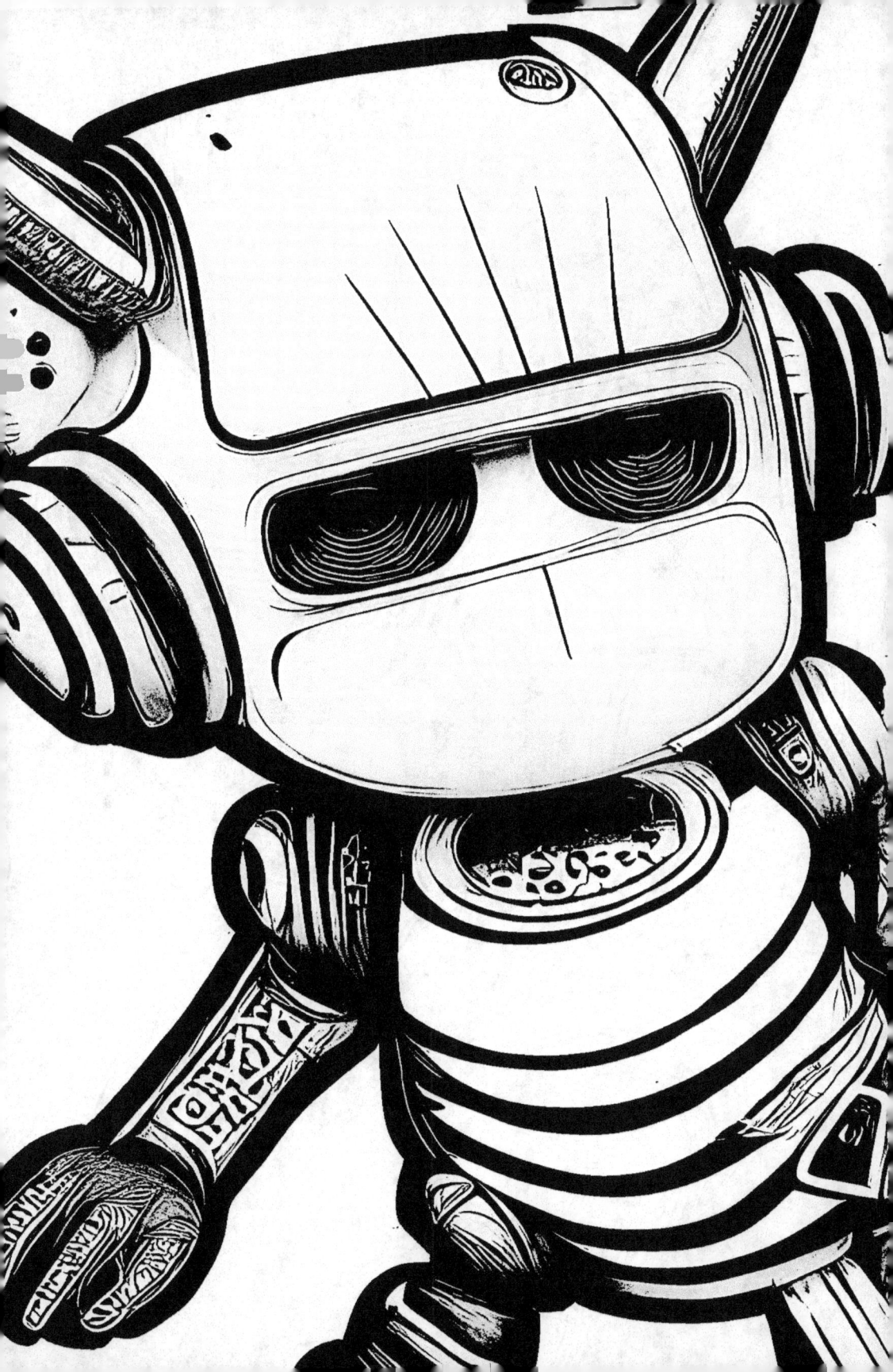

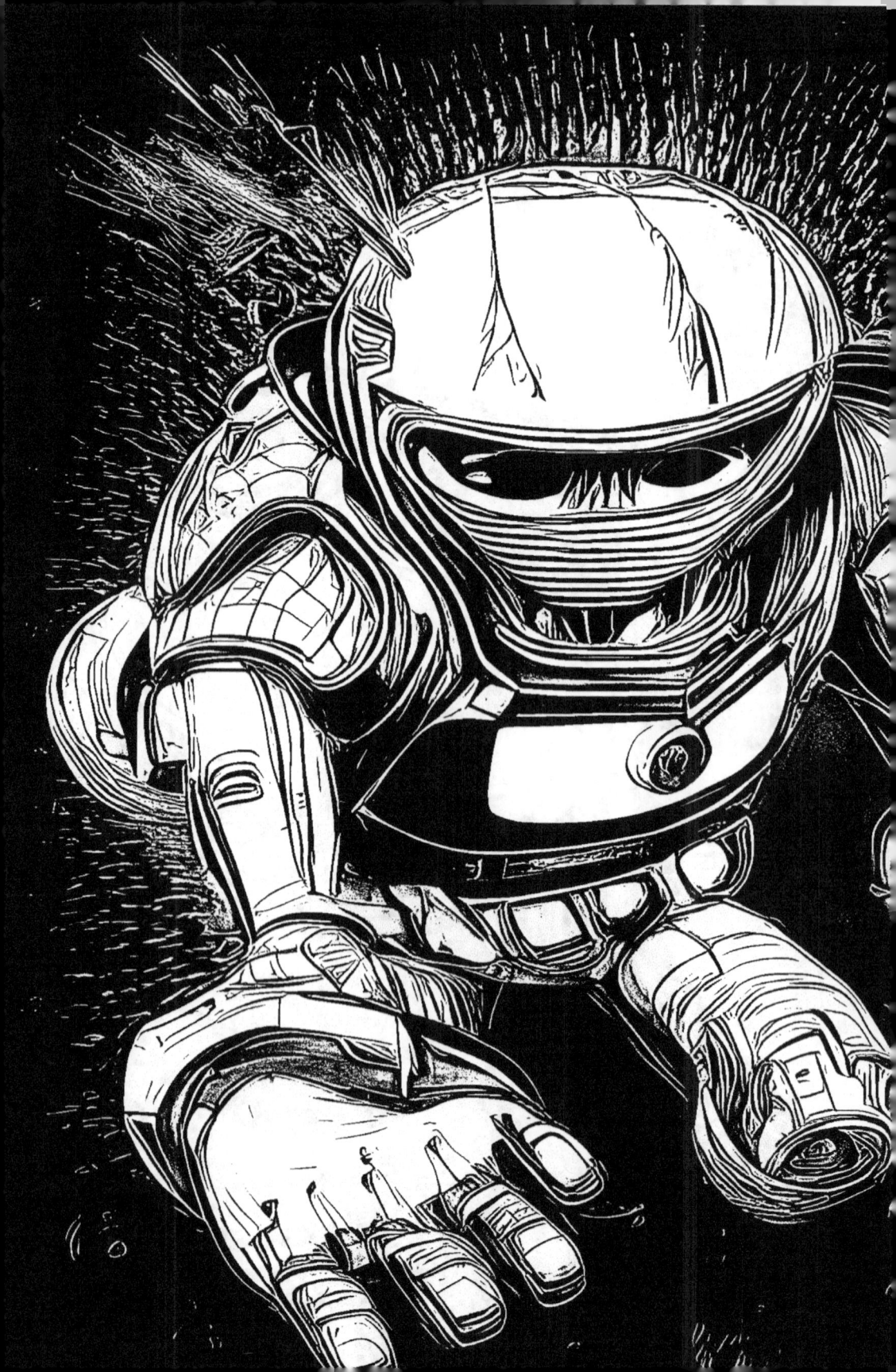

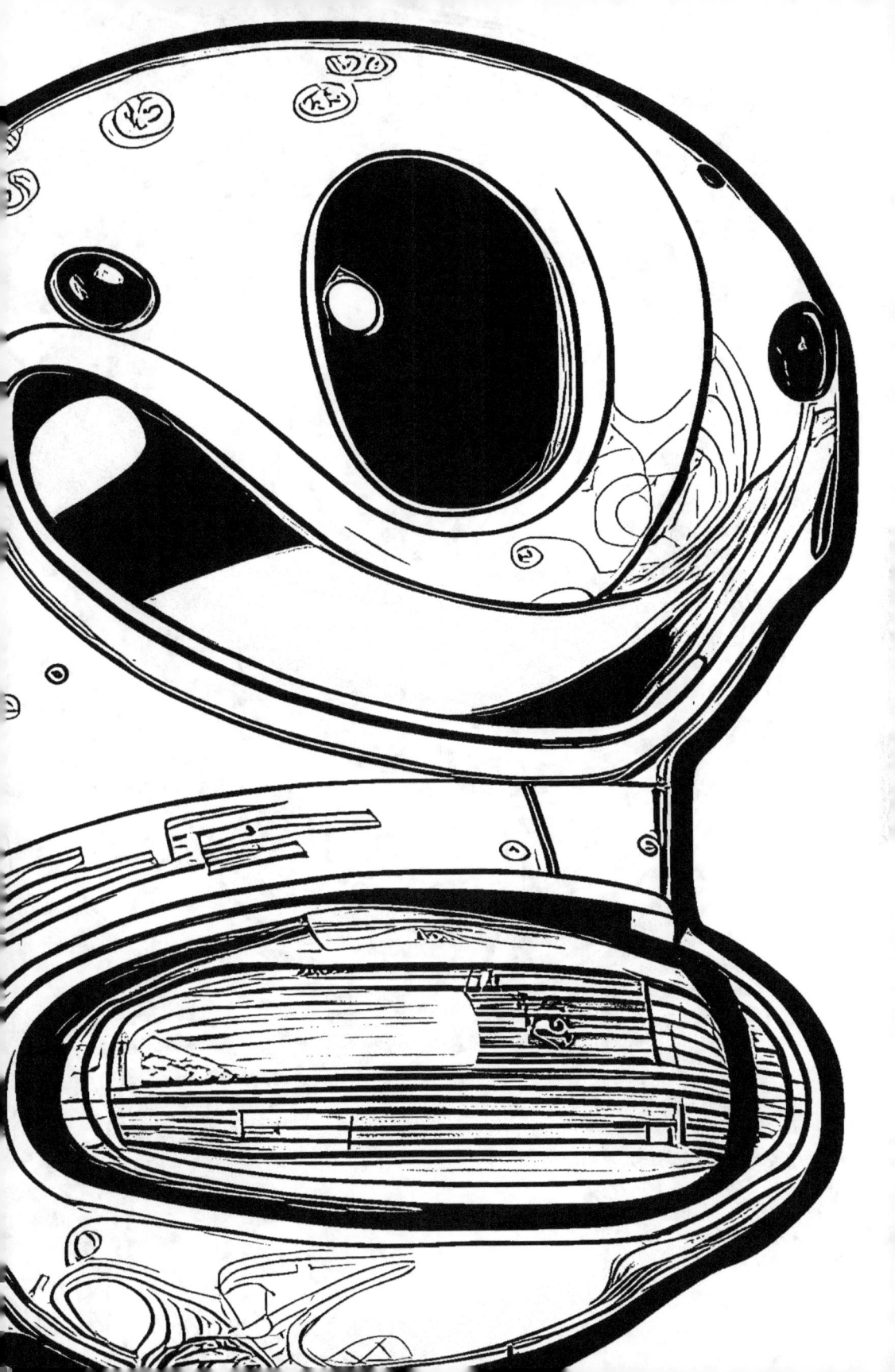

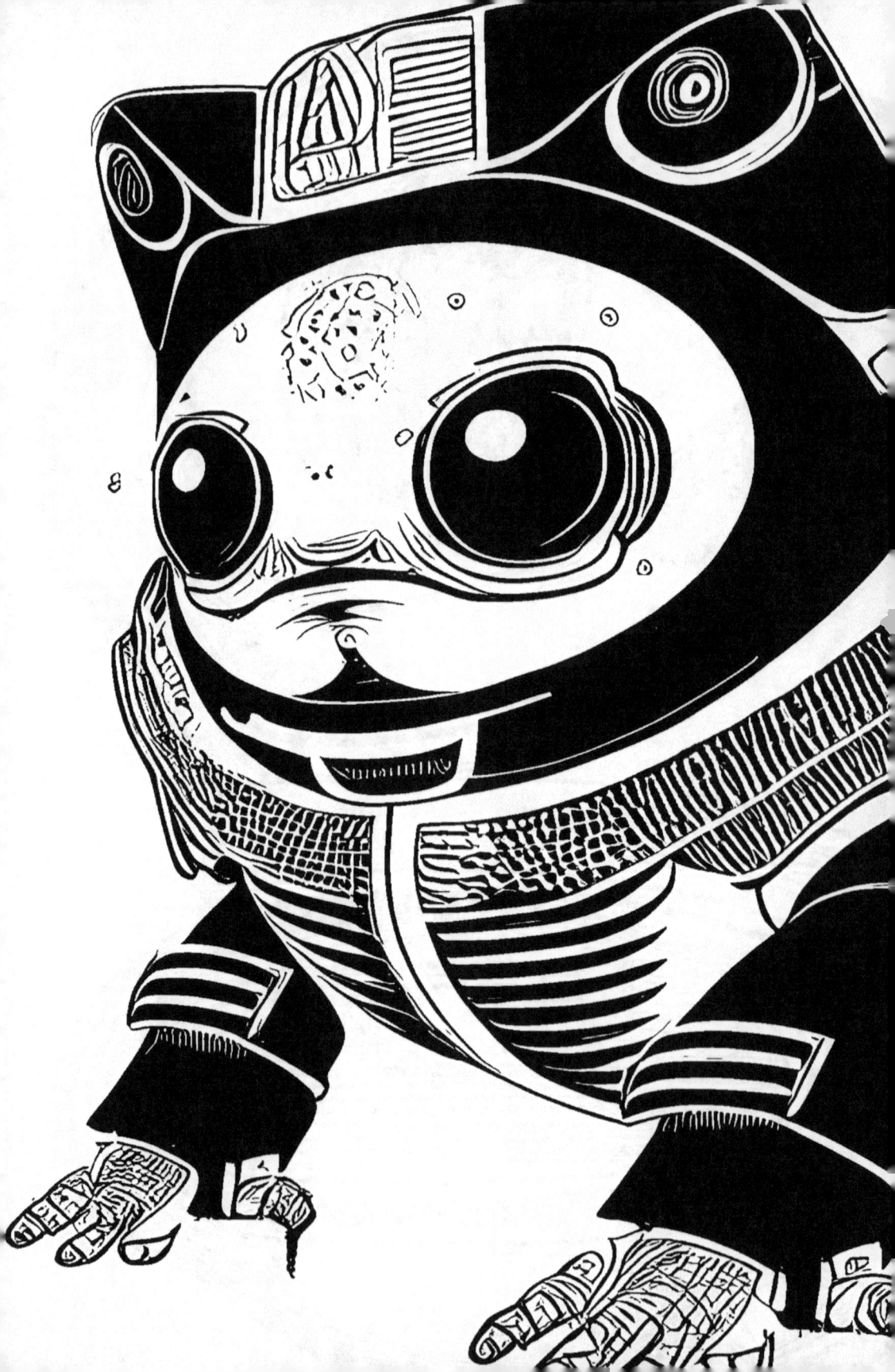

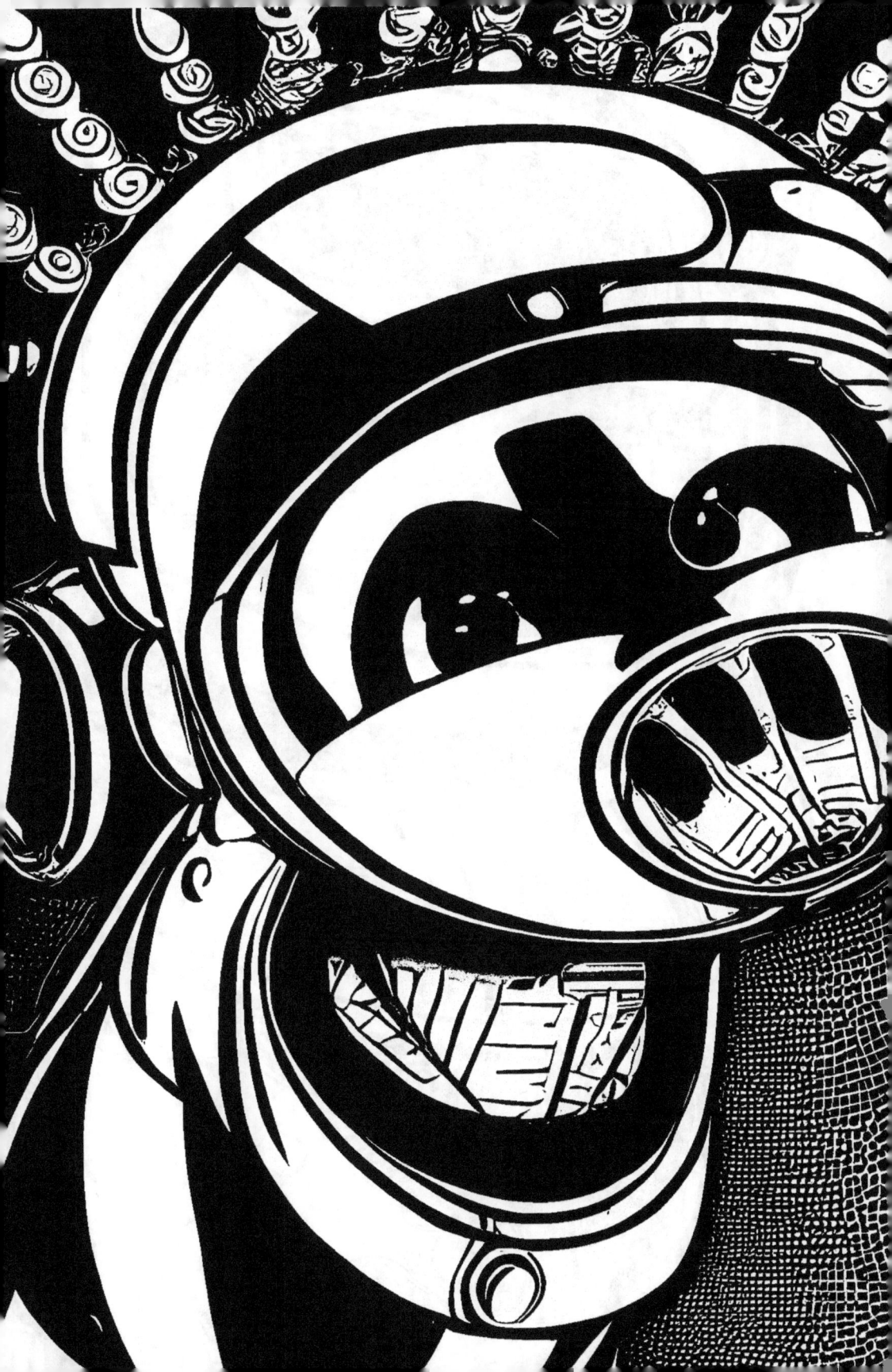

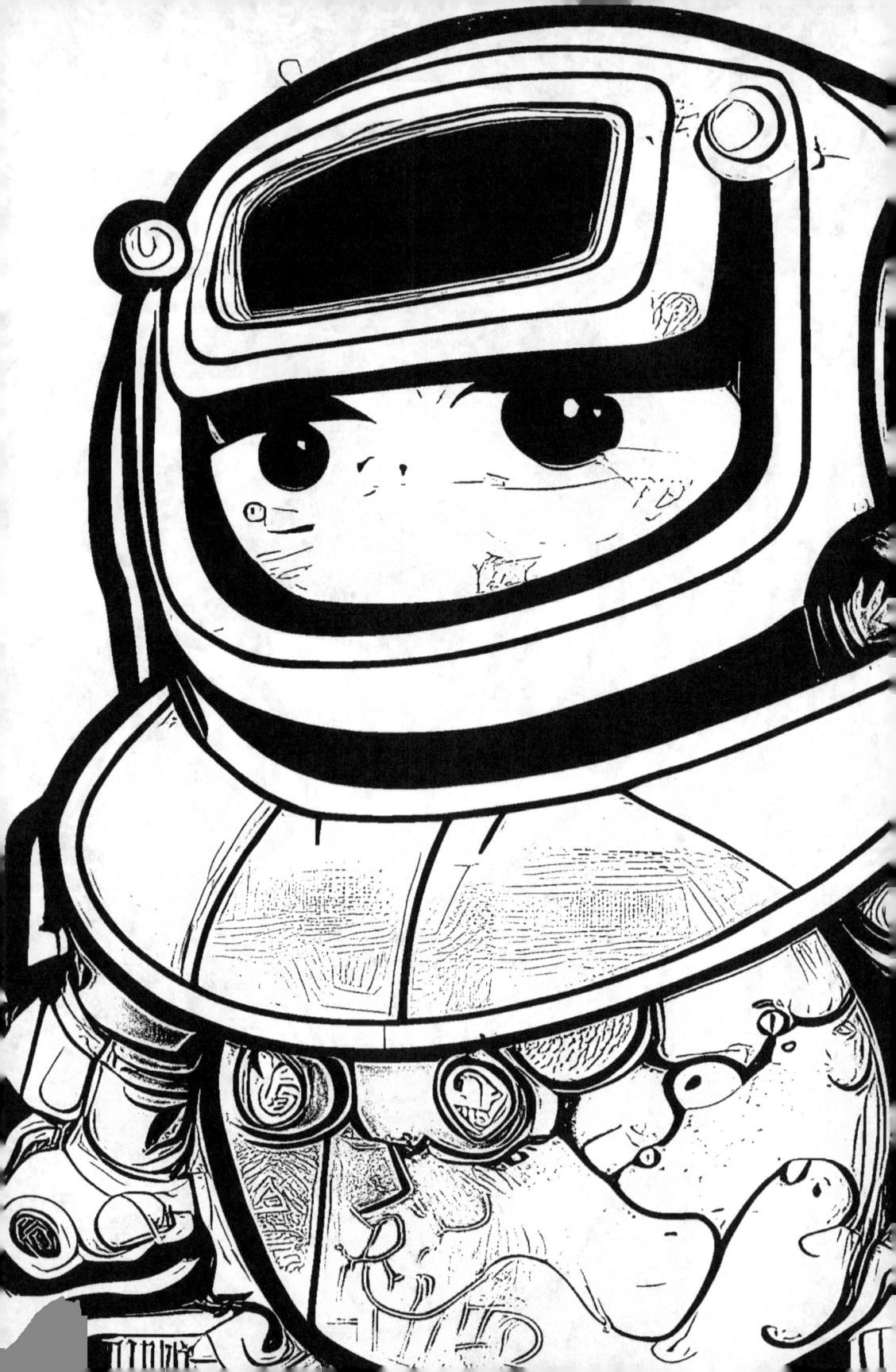

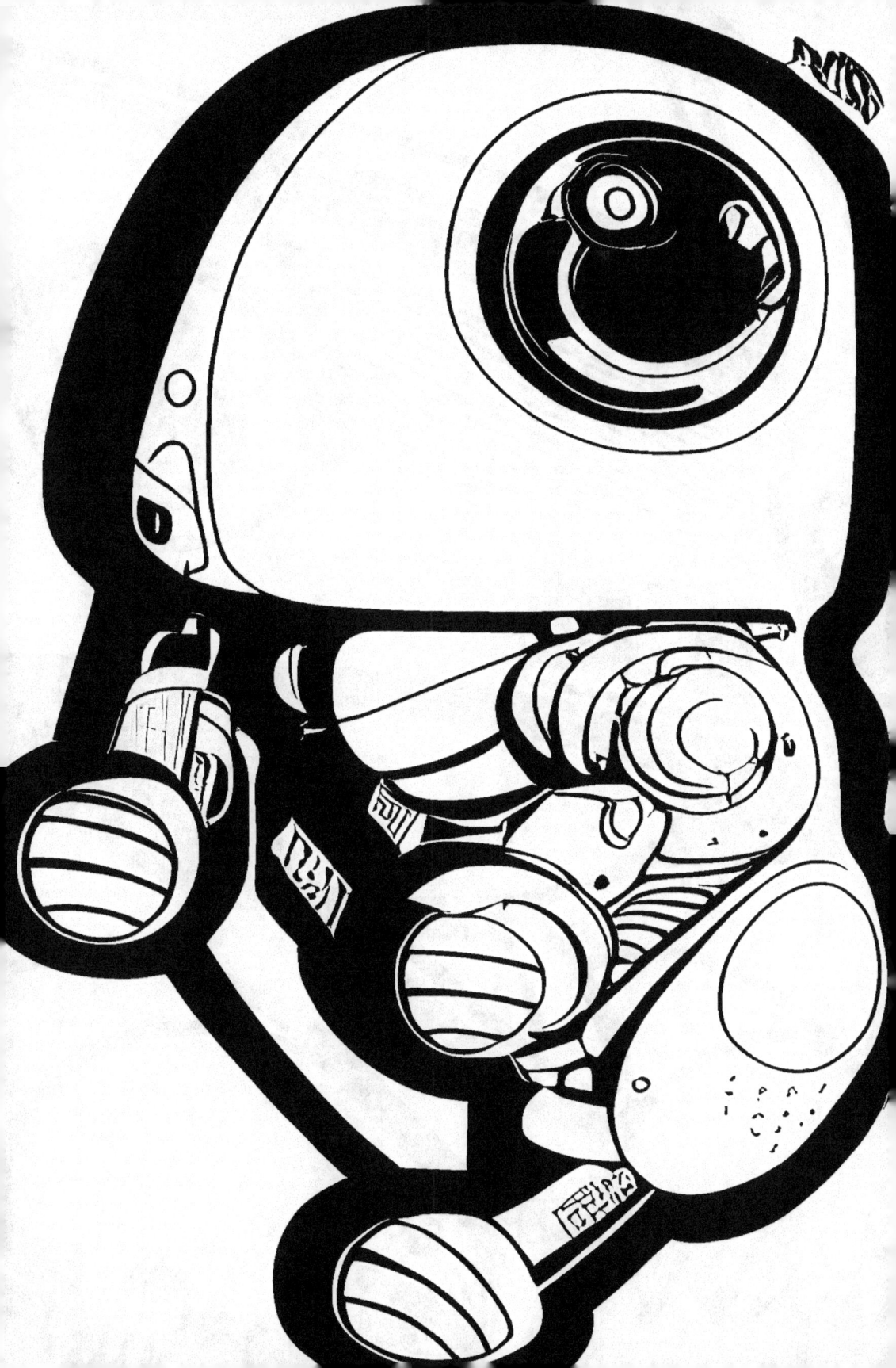

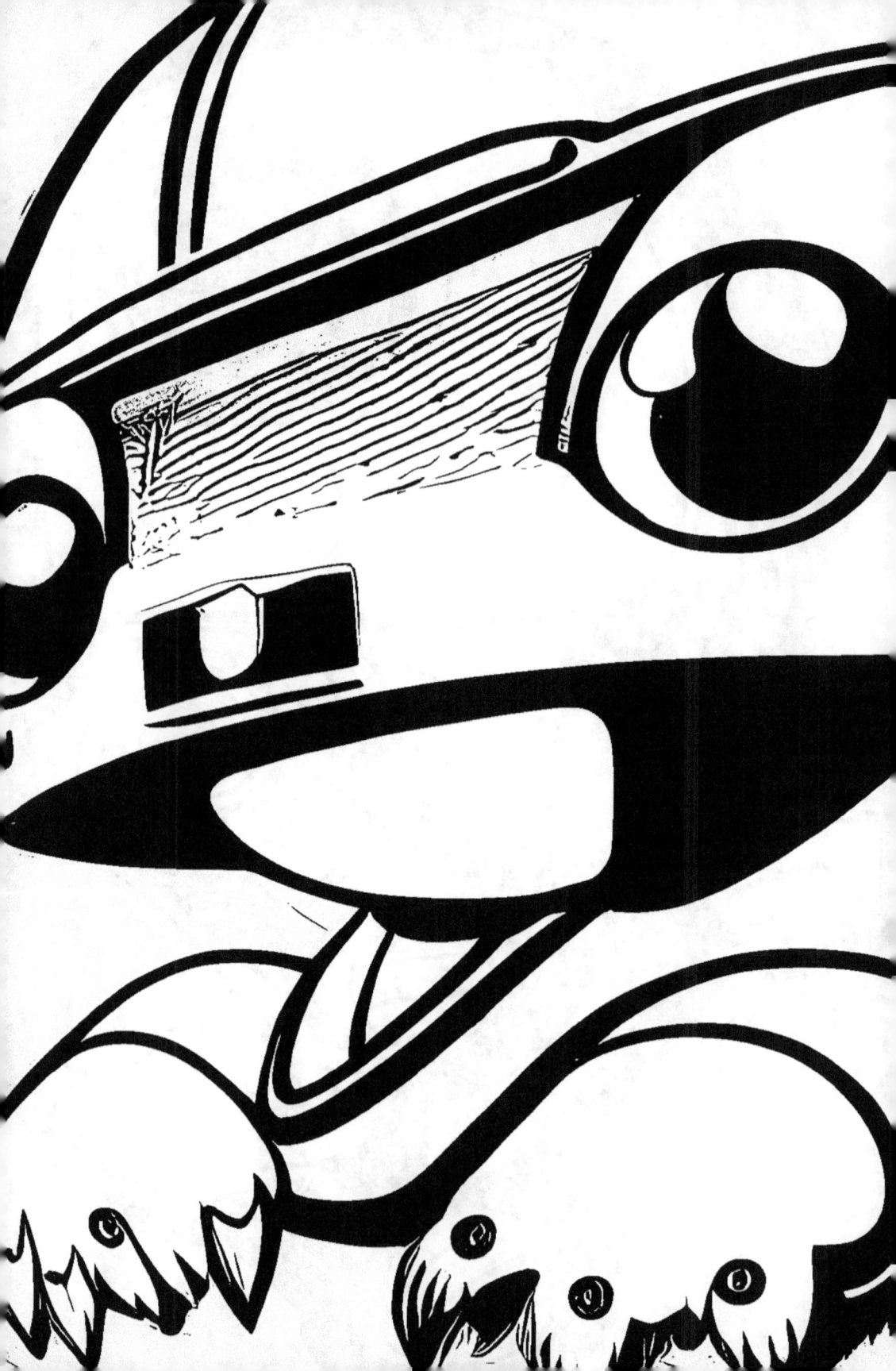

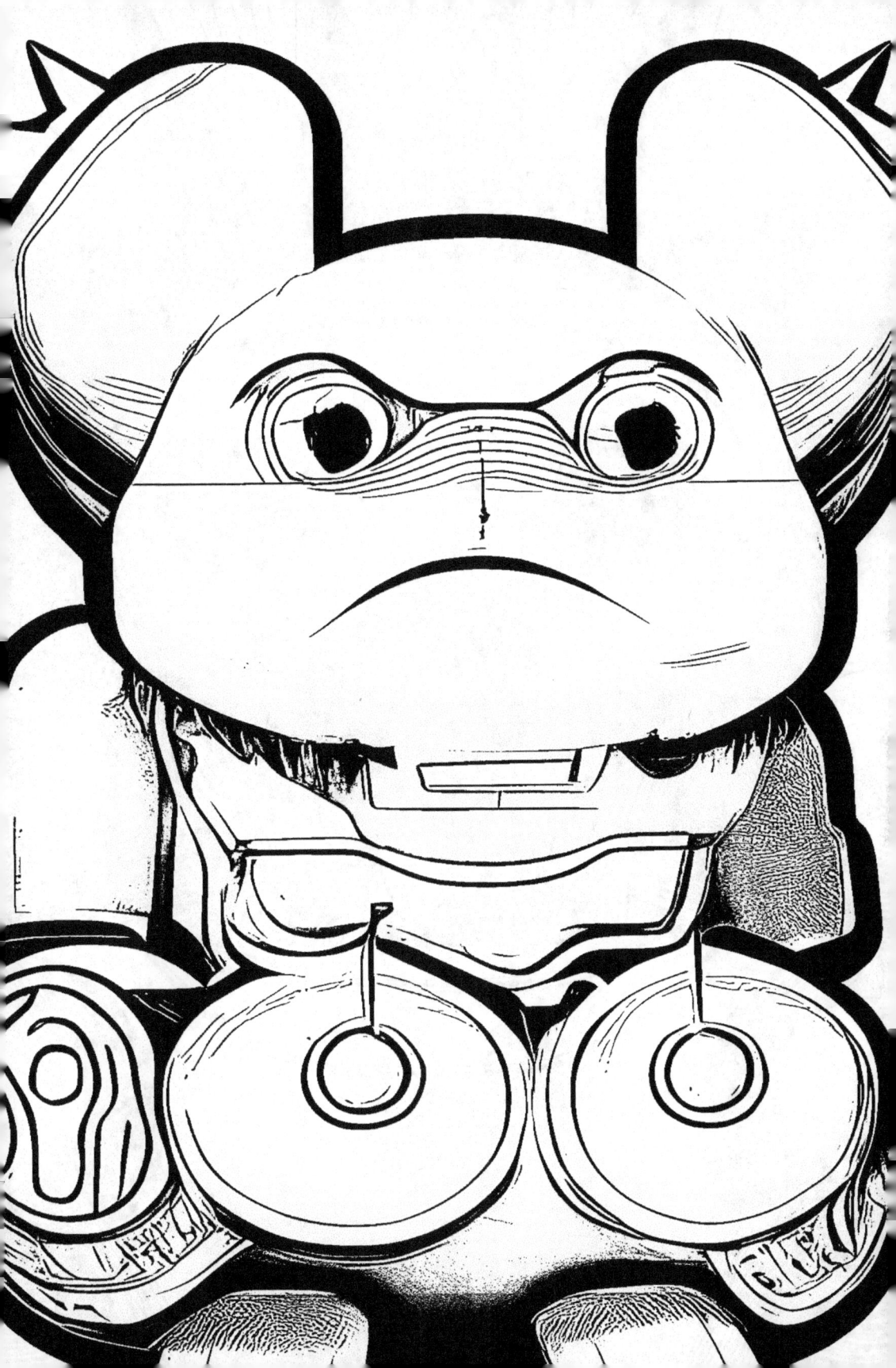

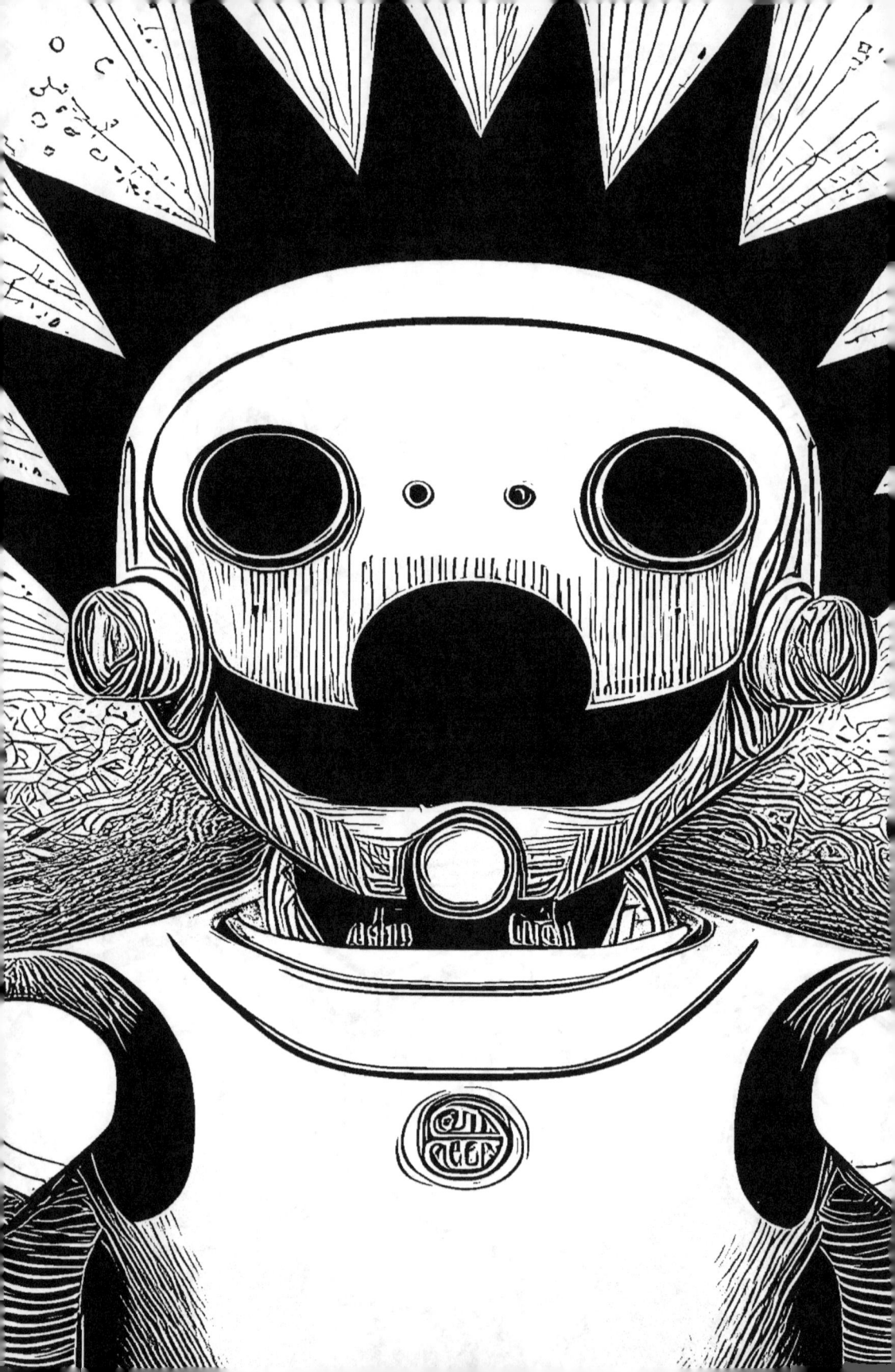

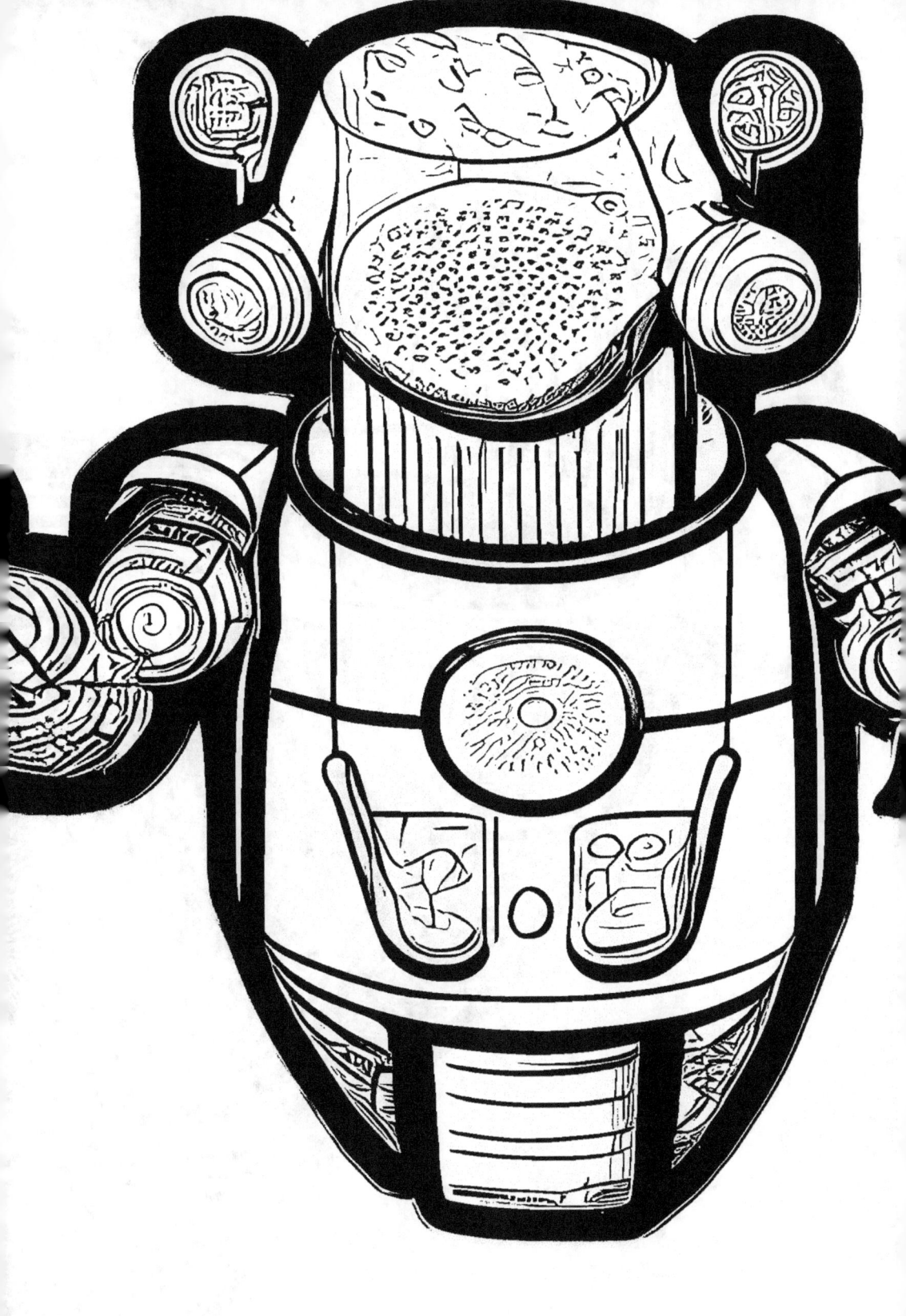

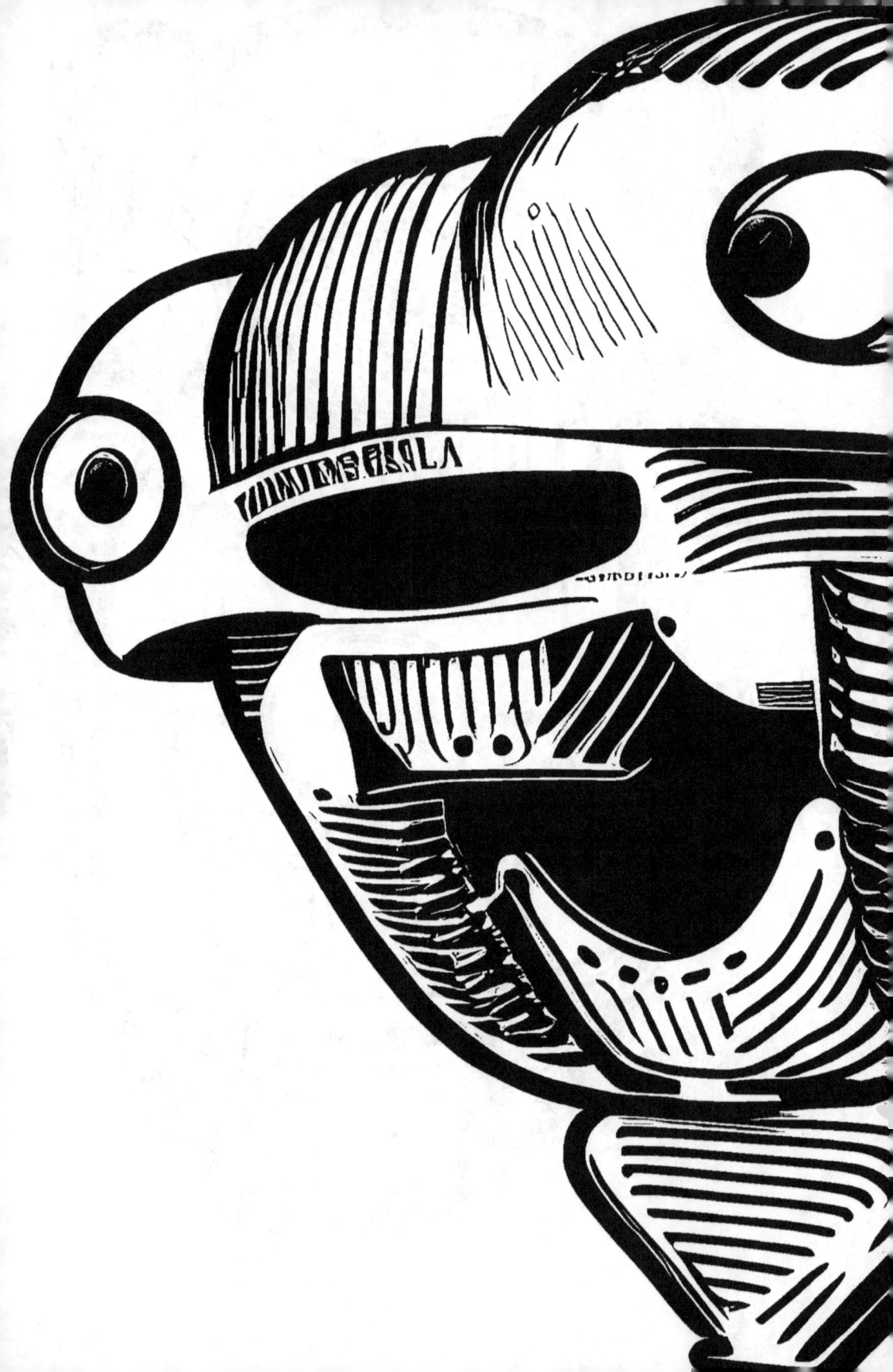

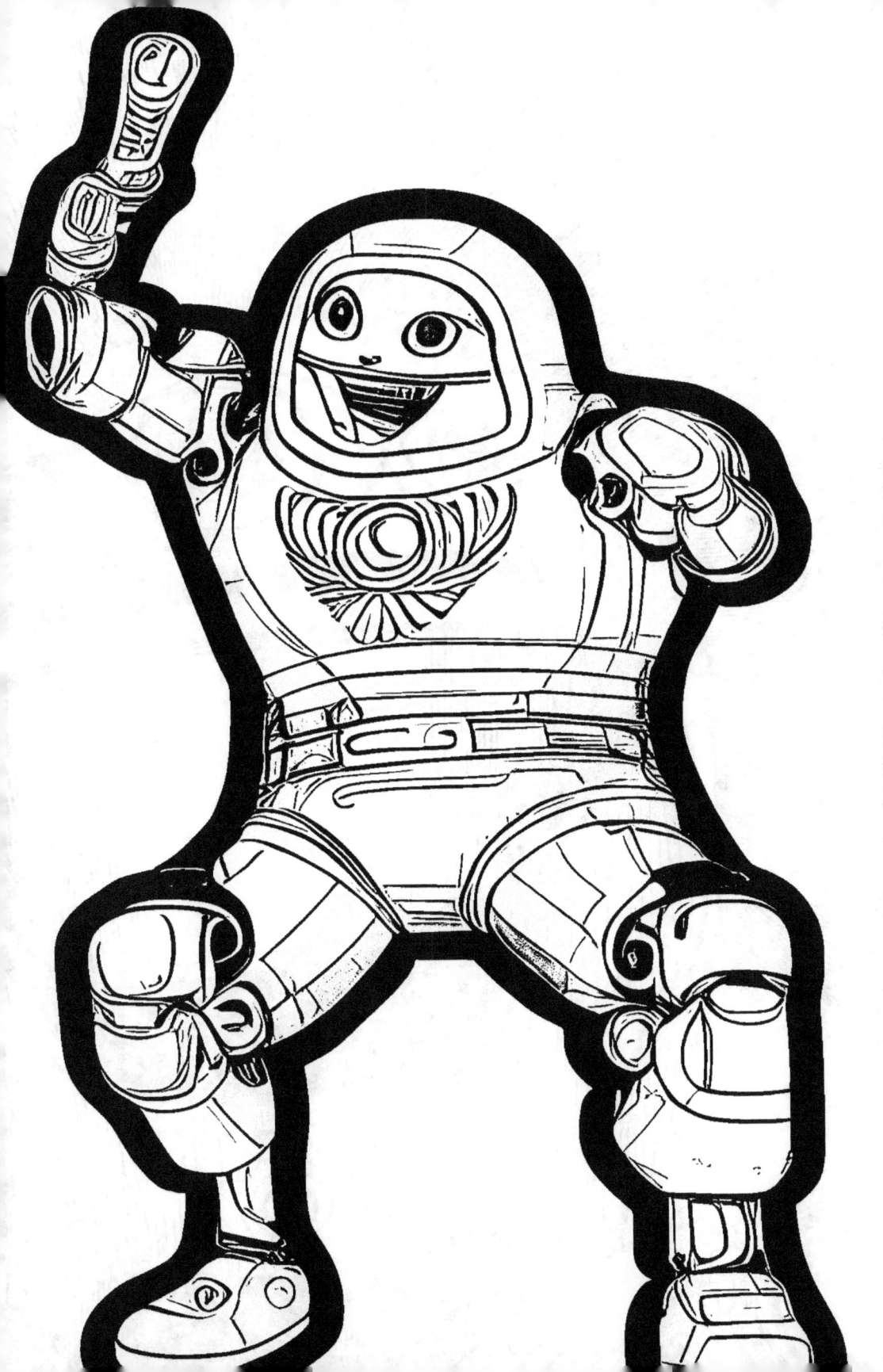

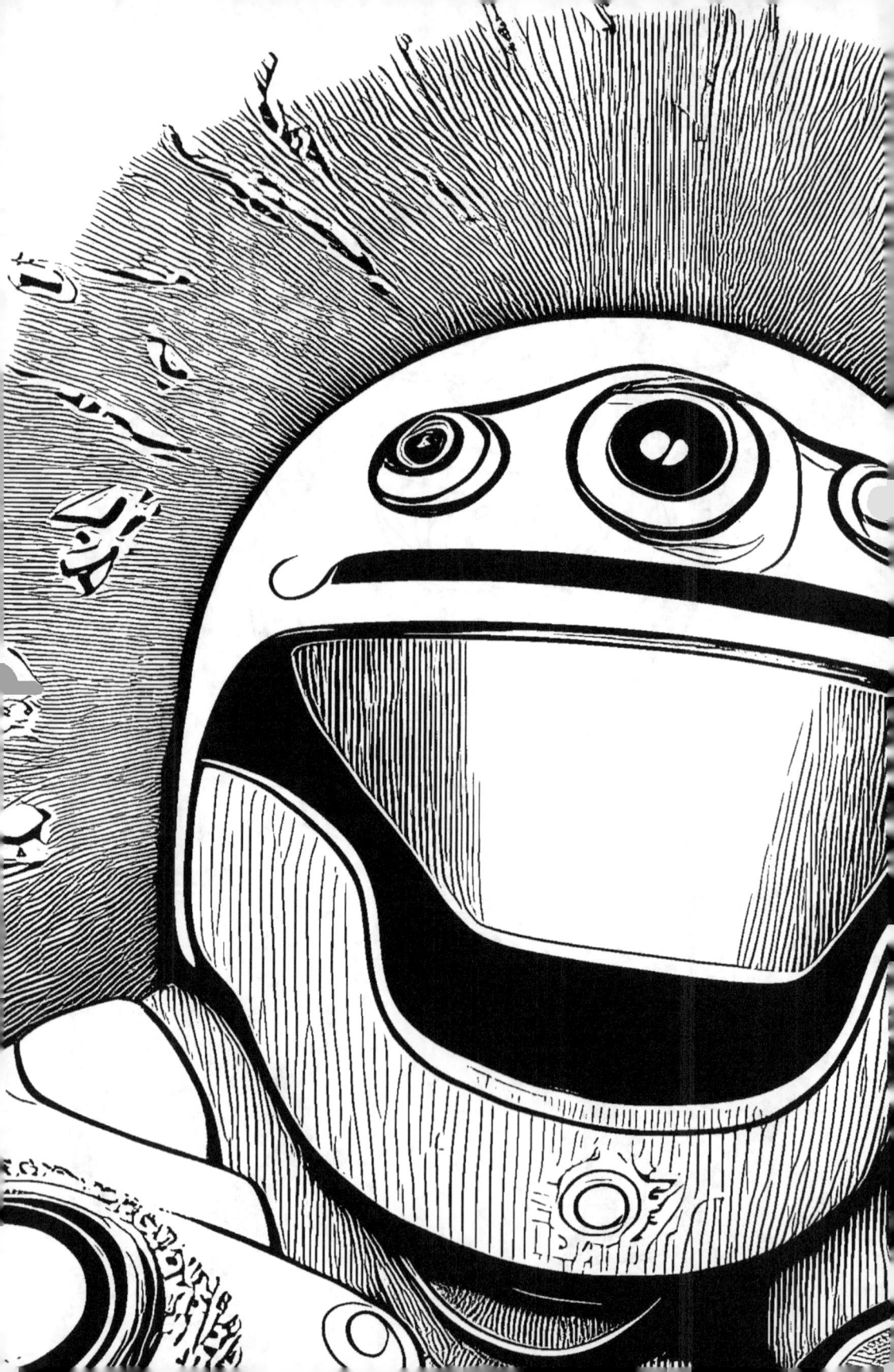

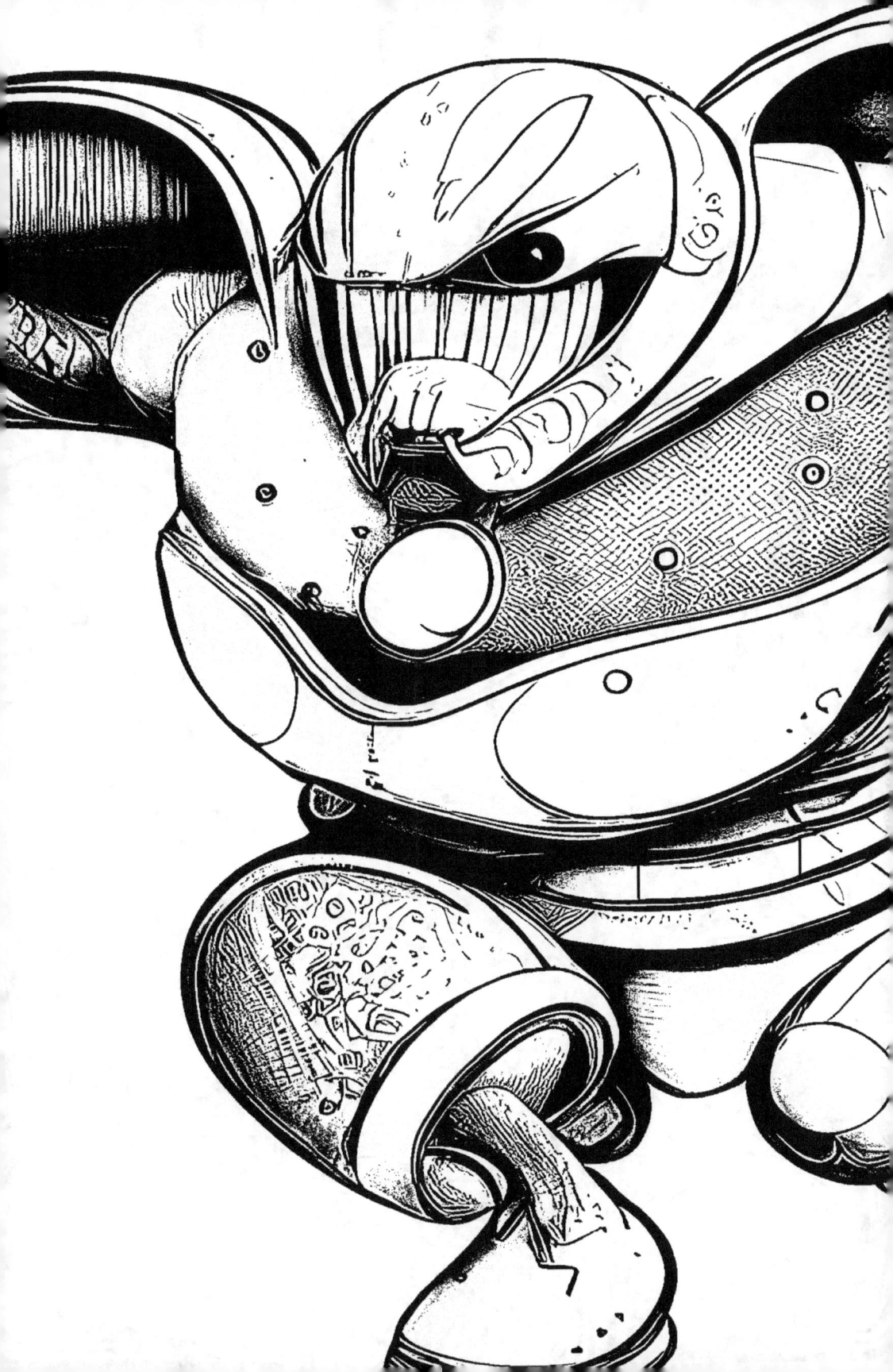

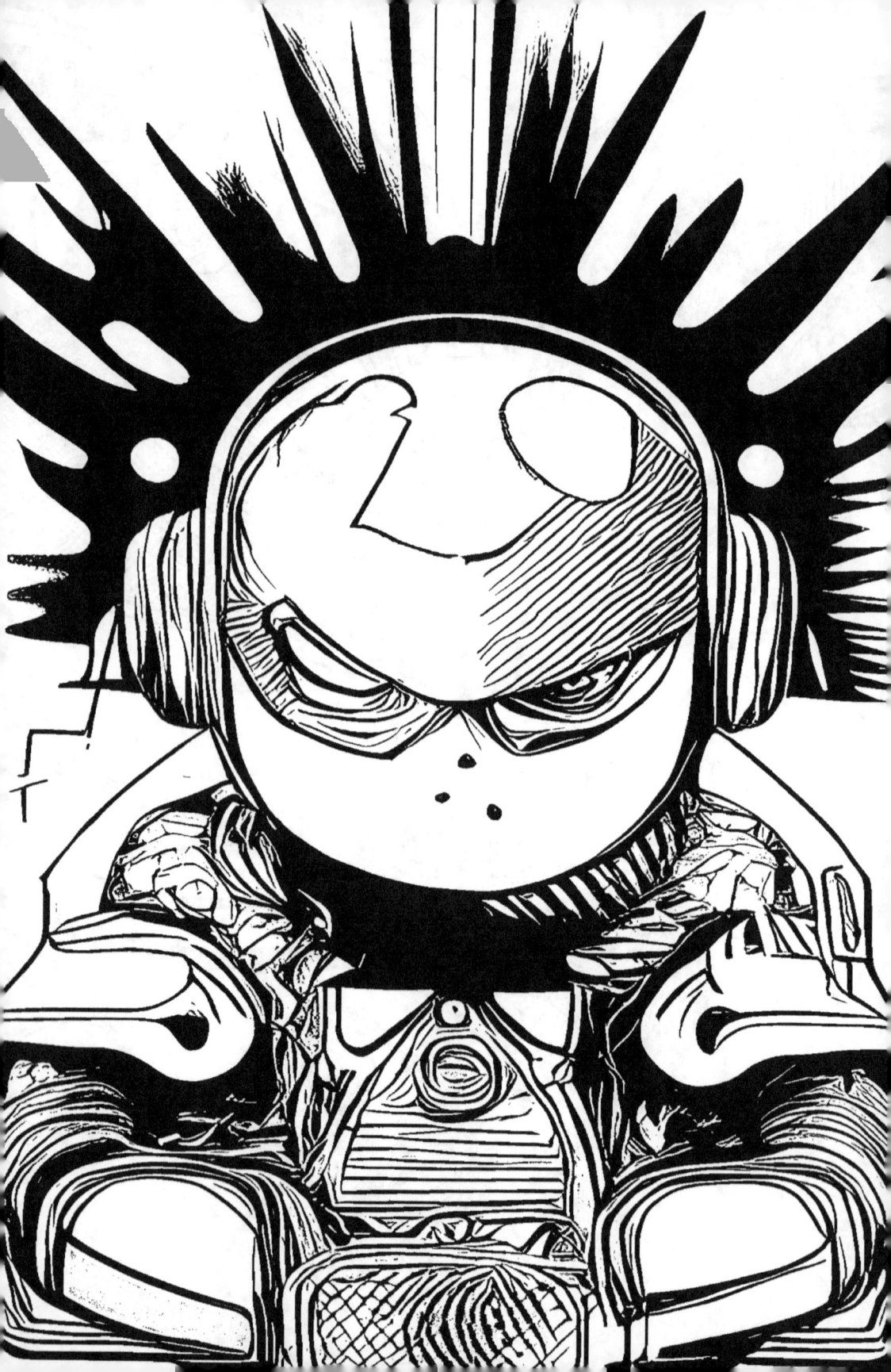

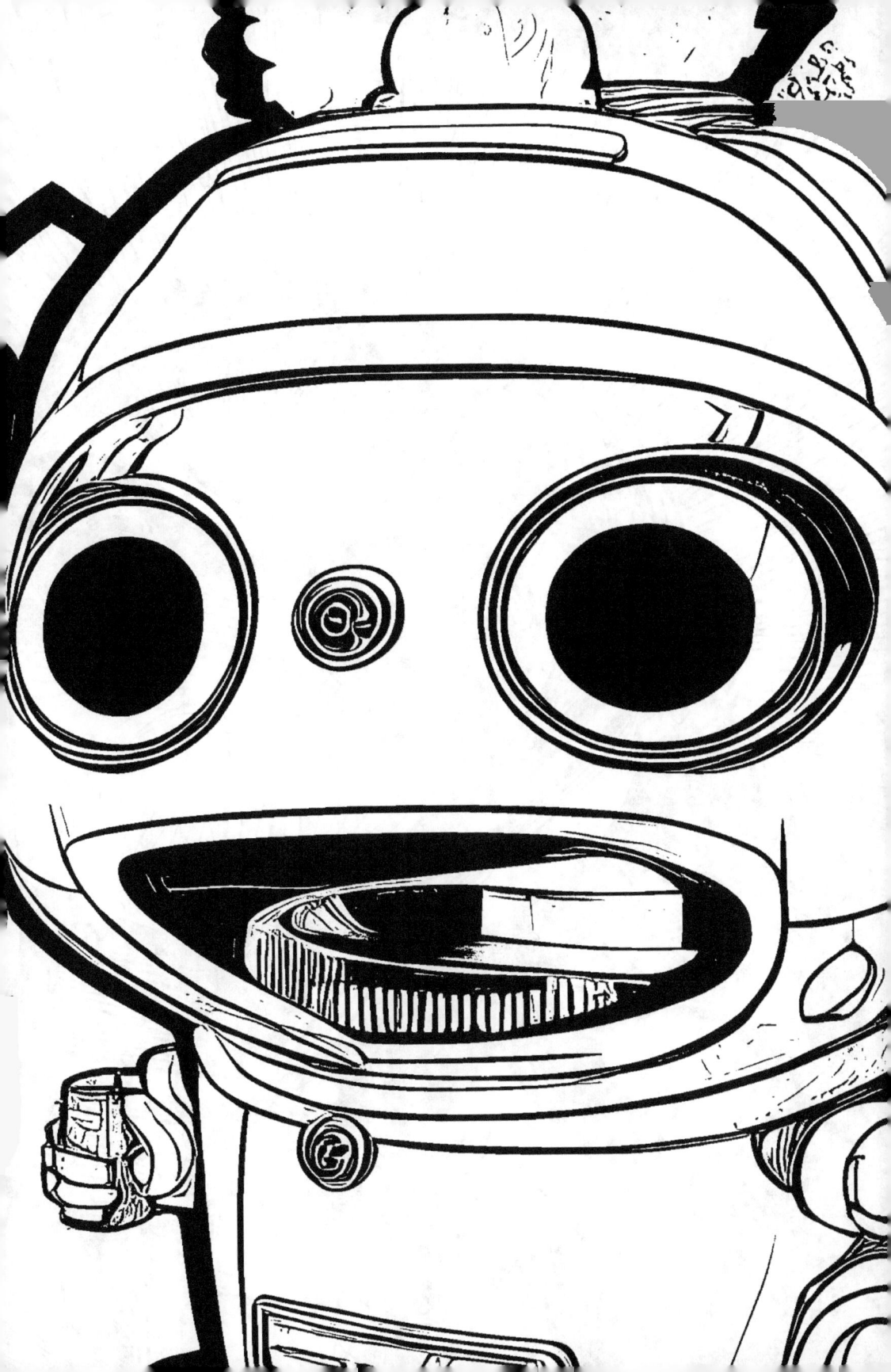

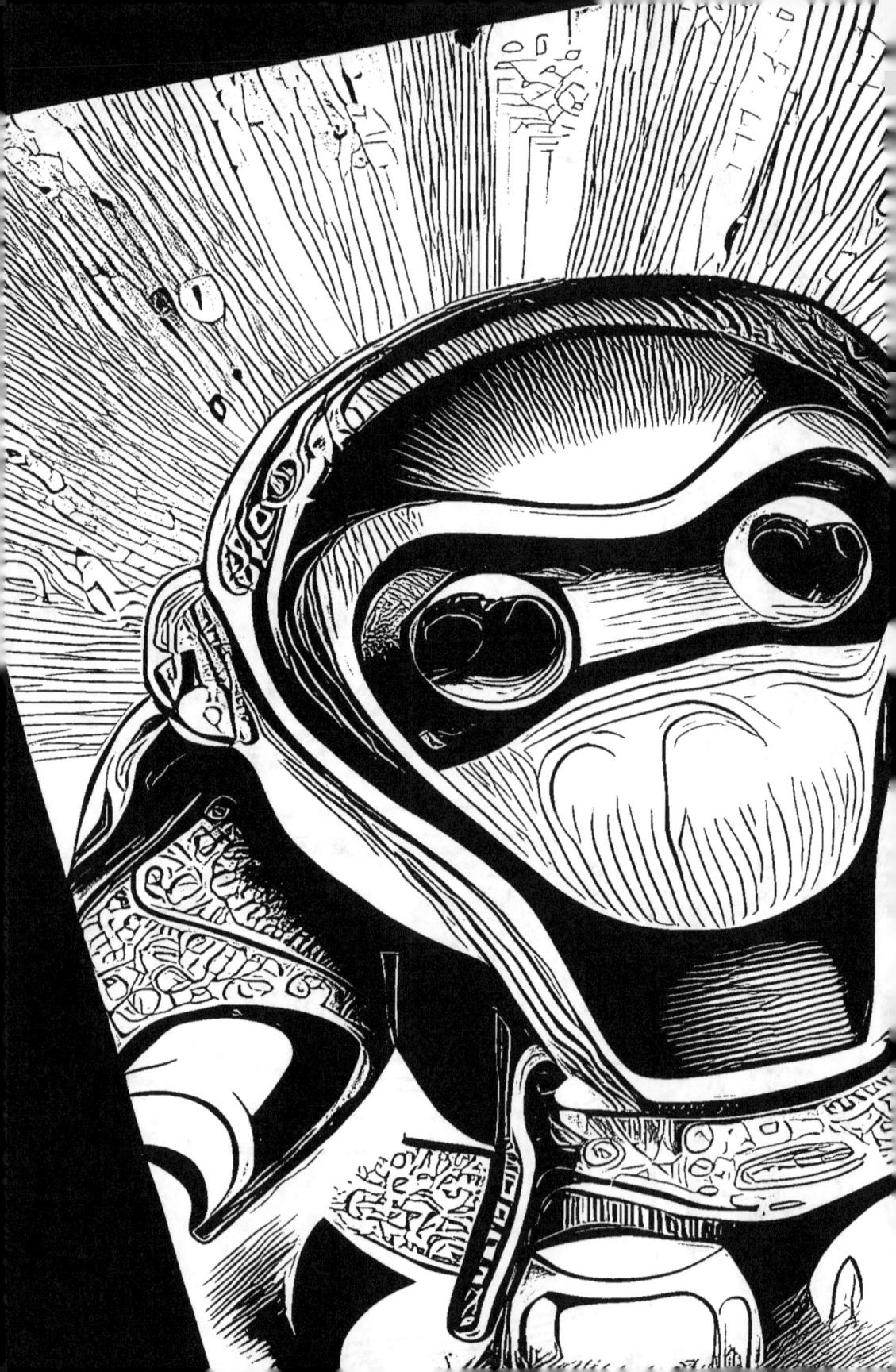

jeremyburt@ishopdailyonline.com

jburt_01@hotmail.com

Make Money Online: https://ishopdailyonline.com

Print On Demand: https://ishopdaily.redbubble.com

Print On Demand @ Etsy: https://ishopdailyonline.etsy.com

dj12mind Instrumental Music Albums: https://dj12mind.com

Affiliate Products: https://index.ishopdailyonline.com

Patreon: https://www.patreon.com/user?u=80194438

Facebook: https://www.facebook.com/jeremy.burt2

Youtube: https://www.youtube.com/channel/UCwV3nApPDh3dNHUGIX4w5nA

tiktok: https://www.tiktok.com/@jeremyburt4?lang=en

amazon: https://www.amazon.com/author/jeremyburt

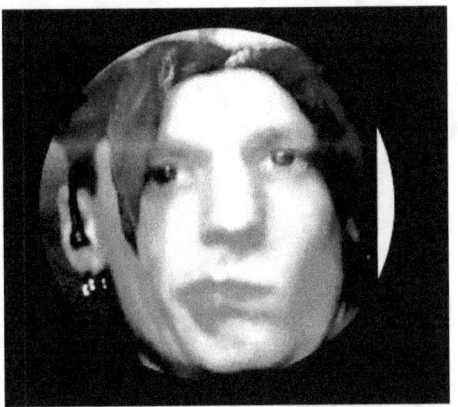

THANK YOU FOR CHECKING IT OUT!

www.ingramcontent.com/pod-product-compliance
Lightning Source LLC
Chambersburg PA
CBHW070911220526
45466CB00005B/2189